Copyright © Kashan Ajmeri 2024

How to Make Money with LinkedIn

Copyright © Kashan Ajmeri 2024

How to Make Money with LinkedIn

Welcome aboard to the world of LinkedIn, where connections transcend borders, opportunities abound, and success stories are waiting to be scripted. If you've ever wondered how a platform primarily known for professional networking can be your gateway to financial prosperity, you're about to embark on an enlightening journey.

Picture this: a bustling digital marketplace where your skills, experiences, and aspirations take center stage. LinkedIn isn't just another social media platform; it's your virtual storefront, your networking powerhouse, and your ticket to the next level of professional and financial achievement.

In this book, "How to Make Money with LinkedIn," we're not here to offer get-rich-quick schemes or hollow promises. Instead, we'll be your trusted guide, unveiling the strategies, techniques, and insider secrets that can transform your LinkedIn presence from a mere profile to a thriving hub of opportunity.

As we dive into the depths of LinkedIn's features and functionalities, you'll discover how to craft a profile that captivates, connect with influencers who can elevate your trajectory, and create content that resonates with your audience. But this book isn't just about accumulating connections or amassing likes; it's about translating those virtual interactions into tangible results.

Whether you're a seasoned professional seeking new avenues for growth, an aspiring entrepreneur eager to carve your niche, or a freelancer looking to expand your clientele, there's something for everyone within these pages. Each chapter is designed to equip you with practical insights, actionable strategies, and real-world examples to empower your LinkedIn journey.

But let's be clear: success on LinkedIn isn't about luck or chance. It's about intentionality, consistency, and a willingness to embrace the dynamic nature of networking in the digital age. So, if you're ready to unlock the full potential of LinkedIn and chart a course towards financial prosperity, turn the page and let's embark on this transformative odyssey together.

Buckle up, dear reader. Your LinkedIn success story starts now.

Introduction: Unleashing the Power of LinkedIn

In today's digital landscape, LinkedIn stands tall as the quintessential platform for professionals worldwide. It's not just a place to list your job history or connect with colleagues; it's a dynamic ecosystem teeming with opportunities waiting to be seized. Welcome to the gateway of your professional and financial aspirations.

Embracing the Digital Marketplace

Picture LinkedIn as a bustling marketplace, where the currency isn't just dollars and cents, but rather connections, collaborations, and career advancements. It's a space where your profile isn't just a virtual resume, but a canvas where you paint your professional narrative for the world to see.

Beyond Networking: A Platform for Growth

Gone are the days when networking meant exchanging business cards at stuffy conferences. LinkedIn transcends geographical boundaries, allowing you to forge meaningful connections with professionals from every corner of the globe. But it's not just about collecting connections; it's about nurturing relationships that can propel your career forward.

The Promise of Possibility

What sets LinkedIn apart is its unparalleled potential to turn possibility into reality. Whether you're a seasoned executive aiming for the C-suite, an entrepreneur with a game-changing idea, or a recent graduate eager to make your mark, LinkedIn offers a level playing field where meritocracy reigns supreme.

Navigating the Terrain

But make no mistake; LinkedIn isn't a magic bullet for success. It's a tool, a platform—a means to an end. To leverage its full potential, you'll need strategy, resilience, and a willingness to adapt to the ever-evolving digital landscape.

What Lies Ahead

In the pages that follow, we'll delve deep into the intricacies of LinkedIn, uncovering hidden gems and practical strategies to elevate your profile from ordinary to outstanding. From crafting a captivating profile to mastering the art of engagement, each chapter will equip you with the knowledge and insights to navigate LinkedIn with confidence and finesse.

Your LinkedIn Journey Begins Here

So, dear reader, fasten your seatbelt and prepare for a journey unlike any other. The path to professional and financial growth awaits, and LinkedIn is your vehicle to get there. Let's embark on this adventure together, armed with curiosity, determination, and a shared vision of success.

Welcome to the world of LinkedIn—a world where possibilities are limitless, and your dreams are within reach.

Chapter 2
Crafting a Killer LinkedIn Profile

In the digital realm, your LinkedIn profile is more than just a digital resume; it's your online persona, your digital storefront, and your first impression on potential employers, clients, and collaborators. In this chapter, we'll unravel the secrets to crafting a LinkedIn profile that commands attention, exudes professionalism, and showcases your expertise in the best possible light.

The Headline: Your Elevator Pitch

Your headline is the first thing people see when they stumble upon your profile, so make it count. Instead of merely listing your job title, infuse it with personality and value proposition. Let it speak to who you are, what you do, and the value you bring to the table.

The About Section: Tell Your Story

Your About section is your opportunity to go beyond the bullet points of your resume and share your story. What drives you? What makes you tick? What unique experiences and perspectives do you bring to the table? Be authentic, be engaging, and don't be afraid to let your personality shine through.

Experience: Show, Don't Just Tell

When listing your professional experience, don't just regurgitate your job descriptions. Instead, highlight your achievements, quantify your impact, and showcase your contributions to your past roles. Use concrete examples and metrics to demonstrate your value proposition and differentiate yourself from the competition.

Skills & Endorsements: Curate Wisely

The Skills & Endorsements section is your chance to showcase your areas of expertise but resist the urge to overinflate your skillset. Be strategic in selecting skills that align with your professional goals and are backed by tangible evidence. And when it comes to endorsements, quality trumps quantity—seek endorsements from credible connections who can vouch for your abilities.

Education & Certifications: Highlight Your Credentials

Your educational background and certifications can bolster your credibility and demonstrate your commitment to continuous learning. Don't just list your degrees and diplomas; highlight any relevant coursework, projects, or honors that showcase your expertise and dedication to your field.

Recommendations: Let Others Sing Your Praises

There's no better validation of your skills and capabilities than glowing recommendations from colleagues, mentors, and clients. Don't hesitate to request recommendations from those who can speak to your strengths and contributions firsthand, and be sure to reciprocate the favor whenever possible.

Media & Publications: Bring Your Profile to Life

LinkedIn allows you to enrich your profile with multimedia content, so take advantage of it. Share links to articles you've written, presentations you've delivered, or projects you've worked on to provide a richer, more immersive experience for visitors to your profile.

Crafting a killer LinkedIn profile is an ongoing process, not a one-time task. Regularly revisit and update your profile to reflect your evolving skills, experiences, and career goals. With a well-crafted profile that showcases your expertise and personality, you'll be well on your way to attracting the right opportunities and making meaningful connections on LinkedIn.

Chapter 3: Building Your LinkedIn Network Strategically

Ah, networking—the cornerstone of professional success. But on LinkedIn, it's not just about collecting connections like trading cards; it's about cultivating meaningful relationships that can open doors, spark collaborations, and propel your career forward. In this chapter, we'll explore techniques for expanding your LinkedIn network strategically, forging connections that matter, and maximizing the opportunities that come your way.

Quality Over Quantity
When it comes to building your LinkedIn network, resist the urge to go on a connection spree. Instead, focus on quality over quantity.

Seek out individuals who align with your professional interests, share your values, or can offer valuable insights and perspectives. Remember, it's not about the size of your network; it's about the depth of your connections.

Personalize Your Invitations

When sending connection requests, take the time to personalize your message. Generic, impersonal invitations are often overlooked or ignored. Instead, mention how you came across the person's profile, why you're interested in connecting, and how you believe you can add value to their network. A little personal touch can go a long way in building rapport and laying the foundation for a meaningful connection.

Engage Authentically

Building a network isn't just about collecting connections; it's about nurturing relationships. Take the time to engage authentically with your connections by liking, commenting, and sharing their posts, congratulating them on their achievements, or reaching out with a thoughtful message now and then. Genuine interactions breed trust and goodwill, laying the groundwork for future collaborations or referrals.

Join Relevant Groups

LinkedIn groups are a goldmine for networking opportunities. Join groups relevant to your industry, interests, or career goals, and actively participate in discussions, share insights, and connect with fellow group members.

Groups provide a platform for exchanging ideas, seeking advice, and building relationships with like-minded professionals who can offer support and guidance along your journey.

Attend Virtual Events

In the age of remote work, virtual events have become the new networking hotspots. Keep an eye out for webinars, workshops, and networking events hosted on LinkedIn, and make it a point to attend and actively participate. Virtual events provide an opportunity to connect with industry experts, thought leaders, and potential collaborators from the comfort of your home —no awkward small talk required.

Offer Value First

When reaching out to new connections or reconnecting with old ones, lead with value. Offer to share relevant resources, introduce them to someone in your network who could be beneficial to them, or provide insights or advice based on your expertise. By demonstrating your willingness to give before you receive, you'll foster goodwill and build stronger, more meaningful connections.

Follow Up and Nurture Relationships

Building a network is just the first step; nurturing those relationships is where the magic happens. Take the time to follow up with your connections periodically, whether it's to congratulate them on a work anniversary, check in on their latest project, or share an interesting article you came across.

Keep the lines of communication open and nurture your connections with care and authenticity.

Building your LinkedIn network strategically is an ongoing process that requires patience, persistence, and a genuine desire to connect with others. By focusing on quality over quantity, engaging authentically, and offering value to your connections, you'll cultivate a network that not only opens doors but also enriches your professional journey in ways you never thought possible.

Chapter 4: Engaging in Content Creation on LinkedIn

Hey there, content creator! Ready to make a splash on LinkedIn? In this chapter, we're diving into the wonderful world of content creation—because let's face it, in today's digital age, content is king. We'll explore strategies for crafting compelling content that not only establishes you as a thought leader but also captivates and engages your audience like never before.

Know Your Audience Inside Out

Before you start crafting content, take a moment to get to know your audience like the back of your hand. What are their pain points, interests, and aspirations? What kind of content resonates with them? By understanding your audience on a deeper level, you can tailor your content to meet their needs and capture their attention.

Educate, Entertain, Inspire

The best content is a blend of education, entertainment, and inspiration. Whether you're sharing industry insights, telling a compelling story, or offering practical tips and advice, aim to strike a balance between informing, entertaining, and uplifting your audience. Keep them coming back for more by delivering value in every piece of content you create.

Be Authentic, Be Yourself

In a sea of content, authenticity is your secret weapon. Don't try to mimic someone else's style or voice; be true to yourself and let your unique personality shine through. Share your experiences, your successes, your failures—whatever makes you, well, you. Authenticity builds trust and rapport with your audience, fostering a deeper connection that transcends the digital realm.

Mix It Up

Variety is the spice of life—and the key to keeping your audience engaged. Experiment with different types of content, from articles and videos to infographics and polls. Mix up your content formats, topics, and styles to keep things fresh and exciting. Don't be afraid to step outside your comfort zone and try something new; you might just stumble upon your next viral hit.

Start Conversations, Spark Dialogues

Content creation isn't just about broadcasting your message; it's about starting conversations and sparking dialogues. Encourage engagement by asking questions, soliciting feedback, and inviting your audience to share their thoughts and experiences. The more you involve your audience in the conversation, the more invested they'll become in your content and your brand.

Consistency Is Key

Building a loyal following takes time and consistency. Commit to regularly publish content—whether it's daily, weekly, or monthly—and stick to it. Consistency not only keeps your audience engaged but also signals to algorithms that you're a reliable source of quality content, potentially boosting your visibility and reach.

Measure, Learn, Iterate

Don't forget to measure the performance of your content and use those insights to inform your future efforts. Pay attention to metrics like engagement rates, click-through rates, and follower growth to gauge what's working and what's not. Then, use that data to refine your content strategy, experiment with new approaches, and continuously improve your content over time.

Creating compelling content on LinkedIn is equal parts art and science. By knowing your audience, staying true to yourself, and experimenting with different formats and styles, you can establish yourself as a thought leader and engage your audience in meaningful conversations that leave a lasting impression.

Chapter 5: Leveraging LinkedIn Groups for Networking

Hey, networking ninja! Ready to take your LinkedIn game to the next level? In this chapter, we're diving headfirst into the wonderful world of LinkedIn groups—a treasure trove of opportunities for expanding your reach, building relationships, and establishing yourself as a force to be reckoned with in your industry.

The Power of Community

LinkedIn groups are more than just digital watering holes; they're vibrant communities buzzing with energy, insights, and opportunities. By joining relevant groups in your industry, niche, or area of interest, you gain access to a network of like-minded professionals who share your passion and enthusiasm.

Expand Your Reach, Amplify Your Voice

One of the greatest benefits of joining LinkedIn groups is the ability to expand your reach and amplify your voice. By participating in group discussions, sharing valuable insights, and engaging with fellow members, you increase your visibility and establish yourself as a thought leader in your field.

Stay Informed, Keep Learning

LinkedIn groups are not just places to network; they're also invaluable sources of knowledge and information. By joining groups relevant to your industry or area of expertise, you gain access to a wealth of insights, trends, and best practices shared by fellow professionals. It's like having a 24/7 think tank at your fingertips!

Forge Meaningful Connections

Networking isn't just about collecting business cards or adding connections on LinkedIn; it's about forging meaningful relationships with people who can support and uplift you on your professional journey. LinkedIn groups provide a fertile ground for building relationships, making new connections, and nurturing existing ones.

Share Your Expertise, Provide Value

One of the best ways to stand out in LinkedIn groups is by sharing your expertise and providing value to fellow members. Share insights, offer advice, and contribute to discussions in a meaningful way. By demonstrating your knowledge and expertise, you'll attract attention, build credibility, and position yourself as a trusted authority in your field.

Be Active, Be Engaged

Like any community, LinkedIn groups thrive on active participation and engagement. Don't be a passive observer; get involved, join conversations, and contribute to the group's discussions. Ask questions, offer solutions, and be genuinely interested in what your fellow group members have to say. The more you engage, the more you'll get out of the group.

Choose Quality Over Quantity

When it comes to joining LinkedIn groups, quality trumps quantity. Instead of joining dozens of groups willy-nilly, focus on a handful of high-quality groups that align with your interests and goals. Choose groups with active engagement, relevant discussions, and members who share your values and aspirations.

Leveraging LinkedIn groups for networking isn't just about adding another item to your to-do list; it's about tapping into a rich ecosystem of opportunities, connections, and insights that can propel your career to new heights. So go ahead, dive into those groups, and watch your network—and your influence—grow by leaps and bounds!

Chapter 6: Utilizing LinkedIn Ads for Business Growth

Hey there, savvy marketer! Ready to level up your game with LinkedIn ads? In this chapter, we're diving deep into the world of LinkedIn advertising—a powerful tool for reaching your target audience, driving engagement, and fueling business growth. So grab your virtual ad hat, because we're about to embark on an exciting journey!

Why LinkedIn Ads?

First things first, why should you consider using LinkedIn ads? Well, for starters, LinkedIn boasts over 700 million professionals worldwide, making it a goldmine for B2B marketers looking to connect with decision-makers and influencers.

With LinkedIn ads, you can precisely target your ideal audience based on criteria like job title, industry, company size, and more, ensuring that your message reaches the right people at the right time.

Understanding the Different Ad Formats

LinkedIn offers a variety of ad formats to suit your marketing objectives and budget. From Sponsored Content and Sponsored email to Text Ads and Dynamic Ads, each format has its unique strengths and capabilities. Take the time to familiarize yourself with the different ad formats and choose the ones that align best with your goals and target audience.

Targeting Your Ideal Audience

The key to successful LinkedIn advertising lies in targeting. With LinkedIn's robust targeting options.

you can narrow down your audience based on criteria such as job title, industry, company size, seniority, interests, and more. Take advantage of LinkedIn's targeting capabilities to hone in on your ideal audience and maximize the effectiveness of your ads.

Crafting Compelling Ad Creative

Once you've identified your target audience, it's time to craft compelling ad creative that grabs attention and drives action. Whether you're creating a Sponsored Content post, a Sponsored InMail message, or a Text Ad, make sure your ad creative is visually appealing, concise, and tailored to resonate with your audience's needs and pain points.

Setting Your Budget and Bidding Strategy

LinkedIn ads operate on a bidding system, where advertisers bid for ad placements based on their chosen targeting criteria. When setting your budget and bidding strategy, consider factors such as your campaign objectives, target audience, and competition. Start with a modest budget and test different bidding strategies to find what works best for your business.

Monitoring and Optimizing Performance

Once your ads are live, the work doesn't stop there. Keep a close eye on your ad performance metrics, such as click-through rate, conversion rate, and cost per conversion. Use this data to identify areas for improvement and optimize your campaigns accordingly. Experiment with different ad creatives, targeting options, and bidding strategies to maximize your ROI.

Iterating and Scaling Up

As you gain insights from your LinkedIn ad campaigns, don't be afraid to iterate and scale up your efforts. Double down on what's working well, whether it's a particular ad format, targeting criteria, or messaging approach. Continuously test and refine your campaigns to drive better results and fuel sustainable business growth.

Utilizing LinkedIn ads for business growth isn't just about boosting your bottom line; it's about forging meaningful connections, driving engagement, and delivering value to your target audience. So roll up your sleeves, dive into the world of LinkedIn advertising, and watch your business soar to new heights!

Chapter 7: Harnessing the Power of LinkedIn Articles

Hey there, aspiring thought leader! Ready to make your mark with LinkedIn articles? In this chapter, we're diving into the wonderful world of long-form content—a powerful tool for sharing insights, showcasing your expertise, and attracting followers on LinkedIn. So grab your virtual pen and let's get writing!

Why LinkedIn Articles?

First things first, why should you bother writing LinkedIn articles? Well, for starters, articles allow you to go beyond the constraints of a typical LinkedIn post and delve deep into topics that matter to you and your audience. Articles are also a great way to establish yourself as a thought leader in your field and build credibility with your network.

Choosing Your Topics Wisely

When it comes to writing LinkedIn articles, content is king. Choose topics that are relevant to your industry, audience, and expertise. Look for gaps in the conversation or emerging trends that you can weigh in on with your unique perspective. Remember, the goal is to provide value to your readers and spark meaningful discussions.

Crafting Compelling Headlines

Your headline is the first thing people see when scrolling through their LinkedIn feed, so make it count. Craft a headline that grabs attention, piques curiosity, and promises value to the reader. Use action words, numbers, and power words to make your headline irresistible and compel readers to click through and read your article.

Writing Engaging Content

When it comes to writing LinkedIn articles, brevity is key. Keep your paragraphs short, and use subheadings, bullet points, and visuals to break up the text and make it more digestible. Write in a conversational tone, and don't be afraid to inject your personality and voice into your writing. Remember, you're not just sharing information; you're telling a story and engaging your audience along the way.

Back-Up Your Claims with Evidence

If you're making bold claims or sharing insights, be sure to back them up with evidence. Cite relevant research studies, statistics, or real-world examples to support your arguments and lend credibility to your writing. Providing evidence not only strengthens your points but also builds trust with your readers.

Include a Call to Action

Every great LinkedIn article ends with a call to action—a clear next step for the reader to take. Whether it's subscribing to your newsletter, downloading a resource, or connecting with you on LinkedIn, make sure your call to action is relevant to the content of your article and encourages further engagement with your brand.

Promote Your Article

Once your article is published, don't just sit back and wait for readers to find it. Promote your article across your social channels, email newsletter, and other relevant platforms to maximize its reach. Tag individuals or organizations mentioned in your article, and engage with readers who leave comments or share your post. The more you promote your article, the more eyes it will reach.

Harnessing the power of LinkedIn articles is a game-changer for establishing thought leadership, sharing insights, and attracting followers on the platform. So don't be shy—pick up that pen (or keyboard) and start writing. Your audience is waiting to hear what you have to say!

Chapter 8: Mastering LinkedIn Messaging Etiquette

Hey there, conversation connoisseur! Ready to master the art of LinkedIn messaging? In this chapter, we're diving into the dos and don'ts of initiating and maintaining professional conversations on LinkedIn. Whether you're reaching out to a potential client, networking with industry peers, or reconnecting with old colleagues, these best practices will ensure you make a positive impression every time.

Personalize Your Messages

When reaching out to someone on LinkedIn, avoid generic, copy-and-paste messages like the plague. Take the time to personalize each message based on the recipient's profile and interests. Mention something you have in common or a specific reason why you're reaching out.

Personalization shows that you've done your homework and genuinely care about building a meaningful connection.

Be Clear and Concise

Nobody likes receiving long-winded, rambling messages, so keep your messages clear, concise, and to the point. Clearly state the purpose of your message in the first few sentences, and avoid unnecessary fluff or jargon. Respect the recipient's time by getting straight to the point and making your message easy to read and understand

Respect Boundaries

While LinkedIn is a professional networking platform, it's important to respect people's boundaries and preferences. If someone doesn't respond to your initial message, don't bombard them with follow-up messages or pester them for a response.
.

Similarly, avoid sending unsolicited sales pitches or promotional messages without first establishing a rapport with the recipient.

Use Proper Grammar and Spelling

Nothing screams unprofessionalism like sloppy grammar and spelling mistakes. Before hitting send on your message, take a moment to proofread it for any errors or typos. Use proper punctuation, grammar, and spelling to convey professionalism and attention to detail. Remember, you only get one chance to make a first impression—make it a good one!

Add Value

When initiating a conversation on LinkedIn, aim to add value to the recipient in some way. Whether it's sharing a relevant article, offering helpful advice, or introducing them to someone in your network, find ways to provide value and demonstrate your expertise. People are more likely to engage with you if they perceive you as a valuable resource rather than a self-promotional spammer.

Be Responsive

If someone reaches out to you on LinkedIn, don't leave them hanging. Be prompt and courteous in your response, even if it's just to acknowledge their message and let them know you'll get back to them later. Avoid leaving messages unread or ignoring them altogether—it reflects poorly on your professionalism and can damage your reputation.

Maintain Professionalism

Above all, maintain professionalism in all your interactions on LinkedIn. Avoid controversial topics, offensive language, or anything else that could potentially tarnish your reputation. Treat everyone with respect and courtesy, regardless of their position or status. Remember, you never know where a conversation on LinkedIn could lead, so always put your best foot forward.

Mastering LinkedIn messaging etiquette is essential for building meaningful connections, fostering professional relationships, and advancing your career. By following these best practices, you'll ensure that every conversation you initiate on LinkedIn leaves a positive impression and moves you one step closer to your goals.

Chapter 9: Showcasing Your Skills with LinkedIn Endorsements and Recommendations

Hey there, skillful professional! Would you be ready to shine a spotlight on your expertise? In this chapter, we're diving into the wonderful world of LinkedIn endorsements and recommendations—a powerful way to showcase your skills, build credibility, and earn the trust of your network. So let's roll up our sleeves and prepare to put our best foot forward!

Understanding Endorsements vs. Recommendations

Before we dive in, let's clarify the difference between endorsements and recommendations. Endorsements are quick, one-click validations of your skills by your connections.

while recommendations are personalized testimonials written by your connections, highlighting your strengths and accomplishments. Both are valuable tools for showcasing your skills and expertise, but recommendations carry more weight due to their personalized nature.

Curating Your Skills

The first step to maximizing the impact of endorsements and recommendations is to curate your skills effectively. Take the time to review and update your list of skills to ensure they accurately reflect your expertise and align with your career goals. Focus on highlighting skills relevant to your current role or desired career path, and remove any outdated or irrelevant skills.

Seeking Endorsements Strategically

When it comes to endorsements, quality trumps quantity. Instead of indiscriminately soliciting endorsements from all your connections, focus on seeking endorsements from individuals who can speak to your skills and expertise firsthand. Reach out to former colleagues, supervisors, or clients who have worked closely with you and can vouch for your abilities.

Giving to Receive

The golden rule of endorsements and recommendations is to give to receive. Before asking for endorsements or recommendations, take the time to endorse and recommend others in your network. Not only does this demonstrate your generosity and willingness to support others, but it also increases the likelihood that they'll reciprocate and endorse or recommend you in return.

Crafting Compelling Recommendations

When requesting recommendations from your connections, be thoughtful and specific in your ask. Provide them with guidance on what you'd like them to highlight in their recommendation, whether it's specific skills, projects you've worked on together, or your overall work ethic and professionalism. The more information you provide, the easier it will be for them to write a compelling recommendation.

Displaying Endorsements and Recommendations

Once you've collected endorsements and recommendations, make sure to prominently display them on your LinkedIn profile. Arrange your endorsed skills in order of relevance and highlight your most impressive recommendations at the top of your profile.

Consider adding a dedicated section to showcase your recommendations, complete with quotes and endorsements from your connections.

Expressing Gratitude

Last but not least, don't forget to express gratitude to those who have endorsed or recommended you. Send a personalized thank-you message to each person who has taken the time to endorse or recommend you, and consider returning the favor by endorsing or recommending them in return. Building a culture of appreciation and reciprocity strengthens your professional relationships and fosters goodwill within your network.

Showcasing your skills with LinkedIn endorsements and recommendations is more than just a vanity exercise—it's a powerful way to build credibility, earn trust, and differentiate yourself in a crowded marketplace. So don't be shy—put yourself out there, highlight your strengths, and let your network sing your praises!

Chapter 10: Creating a Winning LinkedIn Company Page

Hey there, business builder! Ready to make your mark on LinkedIn with a killer company page? In this chapter, we're diving into the ins and outs of creating a winning LinkedIn company page—a powerful tool for showcasing your business, attracting clients, and building your brand presence on the platform. So let's roll up our sleeves and get ready to elevate your company's LinkedIn game!

Establishing Your Company Page

The first step to creating a winning LinkedIn company page is to establish your presence on the platform.

If you haven't already done so, head over to LinkedIn and navigate to the "Create a Company Page" section. Follow the prompts to fill out essential details about your company, such as your company name, industry, size, and website URL.

Crafting Compelling Content

Once your company page is set up, it's time to start creating compelling content that showcases your business and engages your audience. Share updates, news, and insights relevant to your industry, and don't be afraid to inject your company's personality and voice into your posts. Aim to provide value to your followers and foster meaningful interactions with your audience.

Optimizing Your Page for Search

Make sure your company page is optimized for search to increase its visibility on LinkedIn. Use relevant keywords in your company description, headline, and posts to improve your page's discoverability. Additionally, encourage your employees to list your company as their current employer on their LinkedIn profiles, which can boost your page's ranking in search results.

Showcasing Your Products and Services

LinkedIn allows you to showcase your products and services directly on your company page—a valuable opportunity to highlight what sets your business apart from the competition. Take advantage of this feature to provide detailed descriptions, images, and links to your products and services, making it easy for potential clients to learn more and take action.

Engaging Your Audience

Building a thriving LinkedIn community doesn't happen overnight; it requires consistent effort and engagement. Encourage your employees to engage with your company's posts by liking, commenting, and sharing them with their networks. Respond promptly to comments and messages from followers, and actively participate in relevant industry conversations to keep your audience engaged and informed.

Measuring Success and Iterating

As with any marketing initiative, it's essential to measure the success of your LinkedIn company page and make adjustments as needed.

Track key metrics such as follower growth, engagement rates, and click-through rates to gauge the effectiveness of your efforts. Use this data to identify areas for improvement and iterate on your content strategy to achieve better results over time.

Promoting Your Page

Last but not least, don't forget to promote your LinkedIn company page to expand your reach and attract new followers. Share links to your page on other social media channels include a link to your company page in your email signature and marketing materials, and encourage your employees to promote the page to their networks. The more visibility your page receives, the more opportunities you'll have to connect with potential clients and grow your business.

Creating a winning LinkedIn company page is an essential step in establishing your business's presence on the platform and attracting clients. By following these steps and staying consistent with your efforts, you'll position your company for success and unlock new opportunities for growth and engagement.

Chapter 11: Navigating LinkedIn Job Search Like a Pro

Hey there, Career Explorer! Ready to embark on your next professional adventure? In this chapter, we're diving into the world of job searching on LinkedIn—a treasure trove of opportunities waiting to be discovered. Whether you're on the hunt for a new job, exploring career options, or simply curious about what's out there, these strategies will help you navigate your LinkedIn job search like a seasoned pro. So let's dive in and unlock the door to your next big opportunity!

Optimizing Your Profile

Before you start your job search journey on LinkedIn, it's crucial to ensure that your profile is in top-notch shape.

Take the time to update your profile with your latest experience, skills, and achievements. Use keywords relevant to your target role to optimize your profile for search and increase your chances of being discovered by recruiters and hiring managers.

Setting Your Preferences

LinkedIn offers a range of tools and features to help you customize your job search experience. Use the job preferences section to specify your preferred location, industry, job type, and more. You can also set up job alerts to receive notifications when new opportunities that match your criteria are posted.

Exploring Job Listings

Once your preferences are set, it's time to start exploring job listings on LinkedIn. Use the search bar to look for specific roles, companies, or keywords related to your desired job. You can also browse through recommended jobs based on your profile and activity on LinkedIn. Take your time to review each listing carefully, paying attention to the job description, requirements, and company culture.

Engaging with Recruiters

LinkedIn is a networking platform, so don't be afraid to reach out and connect with recruiters or hiring managers at companies you're interested in. Send them a personalized message expressing your interest in their company and inquire about any open positions or upcoming opportunities.

Building relationships with recruiters can help you get your foot in the door and stay top of mind for future opportunities.

Showcasing Your Skills

In addition to applying for jobs, use LinkedIn to showcase your skills and expertise to potential employers. Share relevant content, participate in industry discussions, and engage with thought leaders in your field. The more active and visible you are on LinkedIn, the more likely you are to attract the attention of recruiters and hiring managers.

Use LinkedIn to learn more about the interviewers and their backgrounds, which can help you tailor your responses and make a positive impression during the interview.

Navigating LinkedIn job search like a pro requires a combination of strategy, networking, and preparation. By optimizing your profile, exploring job listings, engaging with recruiters, showcasing your skills, networking like a pro, and preparing for interviews, you'll position yourself for success and unlock new opportunities to advance your career.

Chapter 12: Monetizing Your LinkedIn Presence Through Freelancing

Hey there, freelancer extraordinaire! Ready to turn your LinkedIn profile into a powerhouse for attracting clients and growing your business? In this chapter, we're diving into the world of freelancing on LinkedIn—a goldmine of opportunities just waiting to be tapped into. Whether you're a seasoned freelancer or just starting, these strategies will help you monetize your LinkedIn presence like a pro. So let's roll up our sleeves and get ready to transform your freelance hustle into a thriving business!

Optimizing Your Profile for Freelancing

The first step to monetizing your LinkedIn presence as a freelancer is to optimize your profile for your target audience.

Clearly articulate your skills, expertise, and services offered in your headline, summary, and experience sections. Use relevant keywords that potential clients might search for when looking for freelancers in your niche.

Showcasing Your Portfolio

As a freelancer, your portfolio is your secret weapon for winning clients on LinkedIn. Showcase your best work, projects, and case studies on your profile to demonstrate your skills and expertise. Use multimedia elements like images, videos, and presentations to bring your portfolio to life and make a lasting impression on potential clients.

Networking with Potential Clients

LinkedIn is a networking goldmine for freelancers looking to connect with potential clients. Use advanced search filters to find professionals and companies in your target industry or niche. Send personalized connection requests to introduce yourself and express your interest in working together. Building relationships with potential clients can lead to lucrative freelance opportunities down the line.

Joining Freelance Groups

LinkedIn groups are another valuable resource for freelancers looking to connect with potential clients and peers in their industry. Join freelance groups relevant to your niche or target market and actively participate in discussions and networking opportunities.

Share your insights, offer advice, and engage with other members to establish yourself as a knowledgeable and trusted freelancer.

Publishing Thought Leadership Content

Establishing yourself as a thought leader in your niche is a powerful way to attract clients and grow your freelance business on LinkedIn. Publish articles, posts, and updates that showcase your expertise and provide value to your target audience. Share insights, tips, and best practices that demonstrate your knowledge and position you as a go-to expert in your field.

Seeking Recommendations and Endorsements

Social proof is key to winning clients as a freelancer on LinkedIn. Encourage satisfied clients to leave recommendations and endorsements on your profile to vouch for your skills and professionalism. Displaying positive testimonials from past clients can help build trust and credibility with potential clients who are considering hiring you for their projects.

Promoting Your Services

Don't be afraid to promote your freelance services directly on your LinkedIn profile. Use your headline and summary sections to highlight the services you offer and the benefits of working with you. Share updates and posts about your availability, recent projects, and success stories to keep your network informed and attract new clients to your freelance business.

Monetizing your LinkedIn presence as a freelancer is all about showcasing your skills, building relationships, and positioning yourself as a trusted authority in your niche. By optimizing your profile, showcasing your portfolio, networking with potential clients, joining freelance groups, publishing thought leadership content, seeking recommendations and endorsements, and promoting your services, you'll unlock new opportunities to grow your freelance business and achieve success on LinkedIn.

Chapter 13: Launching Successful LinkedIn Marketing Campaigns

Hey there, marketing maestro! Ready to elevate your brand's presence on LinkedIn and drive real results? In this chapter, we're diving deep into the art of launching successful marketing campaigns on the world's premier professional network. Whether you're promoting a new product, generating leads, or boosting brand awareness, these tactics will help you create and execute campaigns that captivate your audience and drive meaningful engagement. So let's dive in and unlock the secrets to LinkedIn marketing success!

Setting Clear Objectives

Before you dive into creating your LinkedIn marketing campaign, it's essential to define clear objectives and goals.

Are you looking to increase brand awareness, generate leads, drive website traffic, or boost sales? Once you have a clear understanding of what you want to achieve, you can tailor your campaign strategy accordingly and measure your success more effectively.

Knowing Your Audience

Successful marketing campaigns start with a deep understanding of your target audience. Use LinkedIn's robust targeting options to hone in on your ideal customers based on criteria such as job title, industry, company size, seniority, interests, and more. The more targeted your audience, the more relevant and compelling your messaging will be, increasing the likelihood of driving meaningful engagement and conversions.

Crafting Compelling Content

Content is king, even on LinkedIn. Whether you're creating sponsored content, sponsored InMail messages, text ads, or dynamic ads, it's crucial to craft compelling content that resonates with your audience and prompts them to take action. Use eye-catching visuals, concise copy, and clear calls to action to capture attention and drive engagement.

Testing and Optimization

The key to success in LinkedIn marketing is constant testing and optimization. Experiment with different ad formats, messaging strategies, and targeting options to identify what resonates best with your audience. Monitor key performance metrics such as click-through rate, conversion rate, and cost per conversion, and use this data to refine your campaigns and improve your results over time.

Engagement and Interaction

Don't treat LinkedIn marketing as a one-way street. Encourage engagement and interaction with your audience by responding promptly to comments, messages, and inquiries. Join relevant groups and participate in discussions to establish yourself as a knowledgeable authority in your industry. The more you engage with your audience, the more trust and credibility you'll build with potential customers.

Measuring Success

At the end of the day, the success of your LinkedIn marketing campaign boils down to measurable results. Use LinkedIn's built-in analytics tools to track the performance of your campaigns and measure their impact on your business objectives.

Analyze key metrics such as impressions, clicks, conversions, and ROI to gauge the effectiveness of your efforts and make data-driven decisions for future campaigns.

Continuous Improvement

The world of digital marketing is constantly evolving, and what works today may not work tomorrow. Stay ahead of the curve by staying informed about the latest trends, best practices, and platform updates. Continuously iterate and refine your LinkedIn marketing campaigns based on insights and feedback from your audience to ensure you're always delivering maximum value and driving meaningful results.

Launching successful LinkedIn marketing campaigns is equal parts art and science. By setting clear objectives, knowing your audience, crafting compelling content, testing and optimizing your campaigns, encouraging engagement and interaction, measuring success, and continuously improving your approach, you'll unlock the full potential of LinkedIn as a powerful marketing platform for your brand.

Chapter 14: Expanding Your Influence with LinkedIn Live and Video

Hey there, content creator extraordinaire! Ready to take your LinkedIn presence to the next level with the power of live video? In this chapter, we're diving into the world of LinkedIn Live and video content—a dynamic duo for connecting with your audience in a more personal and engaging way. Whether you're a seasoned video pro or just dipping your toes into the live-streaming waters, these tips will help you leverage LinkedIn Live and video content to expand your influence and make a lasting impact on your audience. So grab your camera (or smartphone) and let's dive in!

Understanding the Power of Video

Video is one of the most engaging and effective forms of content on social media, and LinkedIn is no exception.

Video content allows you to convey your message in a more personal and dynamic way, capturing the attention of your audience and fostering deeper connections. Whether it's sharing insights, showcasing products, or hosting live Q&A sessions, video content can help you stand out and make a lasting impression on your LinkedIn network.

Getting Started with LinkedIn Live

LinkedIn Live is a powerful tool for connecting with your audience in real time and sharing your expertise in a live, interactive format. To get started with LinkedIn Live, you'll need to apply for access through the LinkedIn Live broadcasting partner program. Once approved, you can start broadcasting live video content directly to your LinkedIn network, engaging with your audience in real time and fostering meaningful interactions.

Planning Your Content

Before going live on LinkedIn, it's essential to plan your content carefully. Consider your audience's interests and preferences, and choose topics that are relevant and engaging. Whether you're hosting a live interview, conducting a product demo, or sharing industry insights, make sure your content provides value to your viewers and prompts them to participate and engage.

Promoting Your Live Sessions

Once you've planned your live session, it's time to promote it to your LinkedIn network. Share updates and posts about your upcoming live sessions, and encourage your followers to mark their calendars and tune in. Consider using LinkedIn's event feature to create a dedicated event page for your live session, complete with details and reminders for your audience.

Engaging with Your Audience

The beauty of LinkedIn Live is its interactive nature, allowing you to engage with your audience in real time. Encourage viewers to ask questions, share their thoughts, and participate in polls or Q&A sessions during your live broadcast. Respond to comments and questions promptly, and make your viewers feel heard and valued.

Repurposing Your Video Content

Once your live session is over, don't let your video content go to waste. Repurpose your live sessions into shorter, digestible clips or highlight reels that you can share on LinkedIn and other social media platforms. You can also turn your live sessions into blog posts, articles, or podcasts, extending the reach of your content and maximizing its impact.

Measuring Success

As with any marketing initiative, it's essential to measure the success of your LinkedIn Live and video content efforts. Monitor key metrics such as viewership, engagement, and watch time to gauge the effectiveness of your live sessions and video content. Use this data to identify areas for improvement and refine your approach for future broadcasts.

Expanding your influence with LinkedIn Live and video content is a powerful way to connect with your audience in a more personal and engaging way. By understanding the power of video, getting started with LinkedIn Live, planning your content, promoting your live sessions, engaging with your audience, repurposing your video content, and measuring success, you'll unlock new opportunities to expand your influence and make a lasting impact on your LinkedIn network.

Chapter 15: Measuring Success: Tracking and Analyzing Your LinkedIn Performance

Hey there, data-driven dynamo! Ready to uncover the secrets to measuring the success of your LinkedIn efforts? In this chapter, we're diving into the world of tracking and analyzing your LinkedIn performance—a critical step in optimizing your strategy and achieving your goals on the platform. Whether you're a seasoned marketer or just starting on LinkedIn, understanding key metrics and using the right tools will help you gauge the effectiveness of your efforts and make data-driven decisions for future success. So let's roll up our sleeves and dive into the numbers!

Identifying Key Metrics

The first step to measuring success on LinkedIn is identifying the key metrics that align with your goals and objectives.

Depending on your specific goals, these metrics may include:

- Impressions: The number of times your content is displayed on LinkedIn.
- Engagement: Metrics such as likes, comments, shares, and click-through rates.
- Followers: The number of people who follow your LinkedIn page or profile.
- Clicks: The number of clicks on your content, links, or call-to-action buttons.
- Conversion Rate: The percentage of users who take a desired action, such as signing up for a newsletter or downloading a resource.

By focusing on these key metrics, you can gain valuable insights into the performance of your LinkedIn efforts and track your progress toward your goals.

Using LinkedIn Analytics

LinkedIn offers a range of built-in analytics tools to help you track and analyze your performance on the platform. LinkedIn Page Analytics provides insights into your page's performance, including metrics such as impressions, engagement, and follower demographics. Additionally, LinkedIn Content Analytics allows you to track the performance of individual posts and articles, providing valuable insights into what content resonates most with your audience.

Third-Party Analytics Tools

In addition to LinkedIn's built-in analytics tools, there are also a variety of third-party analytics tools available to help you track and analyze your LinkedIn performance.

Tools such as Google Analytics, Buffer, and Hootsuite offer advanced analytics features that can provide deeper insights into your LinkedIn efforts, including website traffic, conversion tracking, and social media ROI.

Setting Benchmarks and Goals

Once you've identified your key metrics and chosen the right tools for tracking and analyzing your LinkedIn performance, it's essential to set benchmarks and goals to measure your progress against. Set realistic, measurable goals for metrics such as engagement, followers, and conversions, and track your performance over time to see how you're progressing toward your objectives.

Iterating and Optimizing

The key to success on LinkedIn is continuous improvement. Use the insights gleaned from your analytics to iterate and optimize your strategy over time. Experiment with different types of content, posting times, and messaging strategies to see what resonates most with your audience. By constantly refining your approach based on data-driven insights, you can maximize the effectiveness of your LinkedIn efforts and achieve better results.

Staying Informed

Finally, stay informed about the latest trends, best practices, and platform updates in the world of LinkedIn marketing. LinkedIn is constantly evolving, and what works today may not work tomorrow.

By staying ahead of the curve and adapting your strategy to reflect changes in the platform and your audience's behavior, you can ensure that your LinkedIn efforts remain effective and impactful.

Measuring success on LinkedIn is all about understanding your goals, tracking the right metrics, and using data-driven insights to optimize your strategy over time. By identifying key metrics, using LinkedIn's built-in analytics tools, leveraging third-party analytics tools, setting benchmarks and goals, iterating and optimizing your approach, and staying informed about industry trends, you'll be well-equipped to measure and maximize your success on LinkedIn.

www.ingramcontent.com/pod-product-compliance
Lightning Source LLC
Chambersburg PA
CBHW070353230526
45471CB00006B/2542